Original title:
Bubbles in the Deep

Copyright © 2025 Creative Arts Management OÜ
All rights reserved.

Author: Fiona Harrington
ISBN HARDBACK: 978-1-80587-407-2
ISBN PAPERBACK: 978-1-80587-877-3

Dreamscapes on the Ocean Floor

Beneath the waves, fish dance and spin,
With goofball grins, they wear a fin.
A seaweed party, what a sight,
Jellyfish jive, under pale moonlight.

Crabs tell jokes with pinch and clap,
While octopuses share a map.
They plan to sail, but who will steer?
Anemones giggle, 'Let's dive, my dear!'

Visions Lost in Liquid Grace

In watery realms where silliness reigns,
A dolphin sings, forgetting its chains.
Turtles impersonate a rock,
While sea cucumbers giggle and mock.

An underwater carnival, quite absurd,
Where squids paint faces with a swirled.
They slip and slide, who'll take the fall?
An elder clam shouts, 'It's all a ball!'

Celestial Droplets of Serenity

Stars twinkle bright beneath the brine,
A crab's ballet, oh how divine!
With coral crowns, they prance around,
Making merry in a frothy ground.

Sea horses laugh as they take flight,
Fins flapping wildly, what a sight!
A floating reef with puns so vast,
Oceanic jesters, having a blast.

The Spectrum of Still Waters

In tranquil tides where giggles float,
A fishy tale, aboard a boat.
An eel jokes, 'I'm not what you think!',
As minnows burst in laughter and wink.

With kelp floats buzzing like a bee,
A playful scene, ever so free.
The currents swirl in joyous cheer,
While crabs in tuxedos declare, 'We're here!'

Murmurs in the Coral Garden

In a meadow of coral, fish do dance,
With fins that wiggle, they take a chance.
A turtle sneezes, bubbles arise,
Creating a rainbow that tickles the eyes.

Seahorses giggle as they twirl and spin,
Chasing their tails with a cheeky grin.
A clam tells a joke, it's truly absurd,
While a starfish chuckles, unheard but stirred.

Dreams Adrift in Stillness

In the calm of the ocean, a jellyfish floats,
Wearing a hat made of tiny, old coats.
A crab with a mirror checks his attire,
While the octopus paints, using ink like fire.

Anemones giggle, swaying to tease,
Tickled by currents, they'd laugh if you please.
The sea cucumbers roll, having a blast,
In a world where silliness happens so fast.

Ethereal Currents of Joy

A dolphin leaps high, splashing with style,
While clownfish pose, with an exaggerated smile.
They're all actors in this watery play,
Chatting in gurgles without words to say.

A narwhal whispers, 'Look at my horn!'
While shrimps clap their claws, their faces all scorned.
With fins that flutter, they spin in delight,
Turning the waves into sheer comic sight.

Crystalline Whirls of the Deep

In the depths of the ocean, where oddities thrive,
A pufferfish giggles, feeling alive.
He shows off his spines like a prickly balloon,
Making all fish laugh, a silly cartoon.

With currents that swirl in a fantastical state,
The whales crack jokes on an underwater date.
Laughter resounds as the sea creatures cheer,
In this world of whimsy, there's nothing to fear.

Vibrations from the Depth

In the ocean's gurgling cheer,
Fish sing tunes that we can't hear.
With a flip and a splash so bright,
They groove beneath the moonlit night.

Crabs in tuxedos dance so bold,
Swapping tales, both funny and old.
A jellyfish glows like a disco ball,
While sea cucumbers plot the prank call!

Whirlpools of Dreaming Light

Whirlpools spin with giggling glee,
Mermaids pulling pranks on me.
Octopuses juggle shells with style,
As I watch, I can't help but smile.

Sea turtles strut like they own the floor,
While seahorses knock on coral's door.
The waves chime in, a comedy crew,
In this underwater rendezvous!

The Art of Subaqueous Reflection

Reflections dance on the waters' face,
A fish does a tap, a graceful race.
Starfish wave like they're on parade,
While coral castles, brightly displayed.

Anemones tickle, and laughter pops,
Plankton floating, never stops.
A crab wearing glasses looks quite astute,
As laughter echoes, what a hoot!

Surface Tension of Memory

Memories dance just like the tide,
In salty air where giggles hide.
Clams tell tales of days gone by,
While schools of fish in suits fly high.

Each drop is a splash of silly fun,
As laughter flickers like the sun.
Remember that time with the dancing eel?
Oh, the joy! It's such a steal!

Colors of the Undersea Symphony

Crabs in tuxedos, dance with glee,
Bright fish in a conga, so carefree.
A starfish strumming on a green guitar,
While seahorses twirl under a candy bar.

Giant clams snort, and the jellyfish sway,
Their shimmering hats drifting far away.
Octopus juggling with shells and snails,
In the carnival of scales and tails.

A turtle comically lost in a hat,
Whispers of laughter crackle and spat.
The anemones clap with their squishy hands,
As laughter bubbles up from the silver sands.

Colorful chaos in the watery hall,
Where the seaweed twirls, inviting us all.
With each playful wave, joy takes a leap,
In this wild world of the ocean's deep.

Tales of Floating Light

A fish in a top hat, with tales to share,
Swims by a crab with a vibrant flare.
Under the sun, they giggle and play,
While the glowing plankton put on a ballet.

Shells hold secrets, each one a prank,
With whispers of wisdom, carved in their plank.
A blowfish puffing, what a silly sight,
As the clownfish jokes about fishy flight.

The rays of the sun cast a shimmering spell,
Lighting up laughter in a seaweed swell.
With each little splash, a giggle follows,
As dolphins dance through shimmering hollows.

Tails trail bubbles, laughter abounds,
In a world of wonder where joy resounds.
Under the waves, the fun never ends,
In the tales of the deep, where the sea life blends.

Enchanted Pools of Serenity

In pools of enchantment, the frogs wear crowns,
Leaping and laughing in lush, green towns.
Seahorses play tag, with tails all entwined,
While they giggle together, perfectly aligned.

The moonlit glow brings a cheerful sight,
As turtles spin yarns of their wild flight.
With every plop and every splash,
A symphony of silliness begins to clash.

An octopus painting with ink from the sea,
Colors of laughter flow so carefree.
Barnacles cheer for the jokes that arise,
While shrimps do the limbo, much to our surprise.

A crab on a skateboard rolls with a twist,
In this world of mirth, who can resist?
With echoes of joy in each carefree leap,
In the enchanted pools, where giggles creep.

Ocean's Secret Symphony

Under the waves, a concert unfolds,
Where fish strum seaweed and octopuses hold.
Fiddler crabs play a jazzy tune,
While bubbles frolic, dancing under the moon.

A whale whispers jokes in a low, deep tone,
Sardines swarm around with giggles overblown.
The starfish applaud with their arms held wide,
As they bask in the laughter the sea can't hide.

The eels do a tango, bold and unique,
While the sea cucumbers sway to the beat.
A jellyfish solo, floating with ease,
Creates laughter like bubbles, dancing in breeze.

In this concert of chaos, hilarity reigns,
As the ocean resounds with whimsical strains.
With each joyful wave, excitement takes flight,
In the ocean's grand symphony, pure delight.

Tidal Dreams in Glassy Depths

Swirling whispers in the blue,
Jellyfish giggle, what a view!
Waves of laughter sprint and leap,
In this sea, no time to sleep.

Seahorses wearing tiny hats,
Dancing with the chatty brats.
Octopus seems full of jest,
Winking eyes, he's quite the best!

Bubblegum fish swim by with glee,
Twisting tails so joyfully.
Crabs cracking jokes, a punny feast,
In this ocean, fun won't cease.

With every wave, a new delight,
Underwater, spirits bright.
In this world of silly games,
Even seaweed has its claims!

Ghosts of Reflection in the Depth

In the shadows, giggles play,
Ghostly figures sway and sway.
Echoes bounce from wall to wall,
A fishy joke, hear the call!

Flapping fins in silly dance,
Haunting dreams just take a chance.
With blank stares, they tell a tale,
Of underwater, vibrant gales!

Phantom bubbles burst with cheer,
Making shadows disappear.
Giggling eels dart to the light,
Turning darkness into bright.

In the depths, a playful haunt,
Whispers of a merry jaunt.
Ghosts and fish in goofy flights,
Mingle through the starry nights!

Luminescent Thoughts in the Abyss

Flickering lights that spark and glow,
Creatures dance in twinkling flow.
Angler fish with funny grins,
Casting light where mischief spins.

Glow sticks gleam from all around,
In this party, fun is found.
Worms in capes, they twist and twirl,
Underwater, oh what a whirl!

Starfish clap and cheer the show,
As playful krill put on a glow.
The sea is full of silly sights,
In its depths, pure delight ignites.

With every flash, a laugh erupts,
In strange hues, the joy erupts.
A tingling thrill in each ray,
Dancing dreams beneath the spray!

The Beauty of Untold Stories Beneath

Tales of treasure hide and seek,
With a wink, a fish might speak.
Clams with pearls, a silly goal,
Fables hidden deep in the shoal.

Crabby critters with tales to weave,
Laughing at what we believe.
Shrimp in a chorus, they sing,
With silly thoughts, they dance and swing.

Secrets swirl like currents flow,
In a world we hardly know.
Each nook and cranny hides a jest,
In the sea's heart, it's truly blessed!

Oh what wonders lie below,
With every bubble, joy will grow.
From tangled weeds to sunken ships,
The ocean shares its funny quips!

The Dance of Airy Orbs

In the water, orbs do sway,
Chasing fish, making play.
Twisting, turning, with a grin,
Who knew fish could join in?

Splish, splash, they bounce about,
Round and round, without a doubt.
An underwater disco ball,
Who knew fish could have a ball?

With every wiggle, every laugh,
They dance, they dash, like a photograph.
In the sun's warm, glowing sheen,
It's a party, what a scene!

Just as we think they'll stop,
They dive and rise — oh, what a drop!
In a gurgling, joyous race,
Come join the fun, it's a silly place!

Shimmering Visions Below

Glimmers flicker in the blue,
What could it be? A fish? A shoe?
They bubble up with a cheeky wink,
Playing games we can't quite think.

Little spheres float oh so near,
What's in there? A fishy beer?
A giggle - this realm is absurd,
Just wait till your senses get stirred!

They tumble down with a silly cheer,
Hiding treasures, never fear.
Let's pop them up, see what's inside,
Oh wait, it's just a fish named Clyde!

In this place of wondrous sights,
They tickle gills and start new fights.
A festival of frothy fun,
Below the waves, under the sun!

Floating Dreams of Yonder

Drifting dreams on bubbly trails,
Whispers of fish with silly tales.
They say in depths, there's laughter bright,
And silly dances every night.

Frothy laughter fills the air,
As fish parade without a care.
In a spiral, they swirl and dip,
With each twist, they bubble and slip.

What's that shimmering in the mist?
A fishy kiss? Or just a tryst?
They giggle as they zoom right by,
Waving fins like clouds on high.

Let the current take you far,
To dreams where finned ones are the stars.
You'll find that joy swims bright and true,
In every wave, a laugh anew!

Eclipsed Inklings in the Tide

In the tide, where inklets play,
Gathering thoughts in a goofy way.
Just who painted the sea so grand?
An artist-fish with a silly hand?

They scribble doodles in the foam,
Each stroke a giggle, far from home.
What's this mess of swirling hues?
Is it art, or just fishy news?

They hide, they seek under the waves,
With secret giggles like playful knaves.
Oh, to join their merry spree,
I'll trade my day for fishy glee!

When the tide rolls into the night,
These inklings dance in pure delight.
With every wave, they leap and glide,
In a world where laughter won't hide!

Secrets that Swim in Stillness

Beneath the calm, fish whisper,
Tales of snacks that make them quiver.
Caught in the net of our small chat,
They giggle at the thought of that.

Seaweed sways with glee, it seems,
Tickling crabs in funny dreams.
Jellyfish play hide and seek,
Each flip a laugh, a playful peek.

An octopus rolls in his ink,
Drawing jokes faster than we think.
With clever tricks, he stirs the tide,
Creating laughter far and wide.

In this world where silence roams,
Even the tides crack silly foams.
For laughter swims in currents bold,
Shared secrets gleam like treasures old.

Liquid Laughter in Depths

In the still, a tickle stirs,
A dolphin's laugh; it softly purrs.
Splashing joy beneath waves bright,
Making ripples dance with delight.

Clams chuckle, pearls plant a grin,
As sea stars do a wiggle spin.
The currents twist, they twist again,
In this realm of ocean's jesting kin.

Anemones wobble, shake with cheer,
Sending giggles far and near.
Each wave a chuckle, each crest a smirk,
As creatures in harmony go berserk.

Beneath the surface, laughter flows,
Where even the shyest fish now shows.
In the depths where snickers play,
Every bubble sings "Hooray!".

The Resonance of Fathomless Dreams

In the depths, a whale hums low,
Echoing secrets where dreams flow.
The sea turtles nod in a trance,
As they witness a bubble dance.

A crab in a tuxedo struts,
Joking with stingrays and their guts.
While snapshots of laughter collide,
In the dreams that the sepia tide provides.

Fish don spectacles, winking bright,
As they giggle through the night.
Tides twist tales of whimsy grand,
Painting smiles in the shifting sand.

In this whimsy, waters gleam,
Debating the nature of the stream.
For laughter echoes, it can't hide,
In fathomless dreams, joy's our guide.

Wishes Adrift in the Ocean

Floating wishes ride the swells,
Hitching hugs from fishy spells.
Ocean waves wear goofy grins,
As laughter leaps and joy begins.

Starfish make plans for a snack,
Sharing stories with a spritz and crack.
Every splash tells a tale anew,
As they dance in bubbles of blue.

At sunset parties, they all gather,
Sea horses talk and yelp and blather.
Each flick of fin sends ripples of cheer,
Celebrating the magic of here.

With every tide, the giggles grow,
As playful currents steal the show.
Wishes ride on frothy streams,
In a world that's woven from dreams.

Fantasies Beneath the Surface.

In a world where fish wear hats,
And octopuses dance like acrobats.
Jellyfish play the trumpet so bright,
While crabs stage a musical night.

Turtles glide, doing the twist,
Seahorses join, they can't resist.
Starfish sing with a splashy cheer,
As the seaweed crowds draw near.

Clams gossip with pearls in their mouths,
Dolphins chuckle at silly spouts.
A squid writes poems with ink in the sea,
While the underwater llama sips herbal tea.

Whales wear glasses and read comic strips,
Sea cucumbers book their trips.
Oh, the laughter, so wild and free,
In this world that's full of glee!

Whispers of the Aquatic Realm

Bubblegum fish swim in a line,
Each trying to look so divine.
They giggle and chase with silly grace,
In a swirling underwater race.

Crabs in bowties throw a grand ball,
While clams on the sidelines just stall.
The anchorfish swaps tales of the sea,
While anemones laugh, feeling so free.

Jellys do pirouettes on the floor,
Shiny scales glimmer, who could ask for more?
One jellybean fish says, 'What a sight!'
As clownfish juggle, oh what delight!

With seaweed wigs and shimmering lights,
Creatures dance through the ocean nights.
In this realm, so funny and bright,
Every day is a whimsical flight!

Echoes Beneath the Surface

Whales tell jokes in a sonorous way,
As minnows giggle and join in the play.
Anemones sway to the rhythm so fine,
While seahorses plan a grand line dance design.

A hermit crab wears a shiny new shoe,
While fish debate which shade of blue.
Starfish spin like a top on a dare,
While sardines form a conga affair.

Clownfish crack up at their own silly faces,
In the coral, they twirl through the spaces.
Fiddler crabs hold a talent show,
Where the winner gets to wear a bow!

Unexpected splashes and giggles abound,
As laughter echoes all around.
In these depths, where humor reigns,
Ocean's joy is caught in the chains!

Dreams of the Sunken Sea

Mermaids dream of pizza and cake,
While sea slugs plot their charming break.
With bubble wrap shells, they float with glee,
In a treasure chest under a big sea tree.

Giant squids run a circus of fun,
With seals on unicycles, oh what a run!
Pufferfish juggle with ease and delight,
As eels crack jokes in the pale moonlight.

Crabs have a picnic with starfruit to share,
While lobsters giggle without a care.
In this world where laughter seems key,
The secret to life's in the briny spree.

Dolphins hold court, they sip on the tide,
In their world, they never do hide.
With each splash, joy is ever so near,
In their sunken dreams, there's nothing to fear!

Ethereal Orbs of the Abyss

In the depths where giggles float,
Silly spheres sail, like a boat.
They wiggle and dance with such grace,
Making fish laugh at their silly face.

A jellyfish jokes with a wink,
While the shy seaweed starts to think.
A crab in a tux takes a bow,
Crowning the show, oh take a vow!

Tiny bright pearls make a show,
Juggling water, to and fro.
The eel sneezes, the crowd erupts,
In flowing laughs, the silence erupts.

The octopus twirls, wearing a hat,
As sea turtles cheer for the acrobat.
In the realm where joy never sleeps,
Lives the secret of giggles that leaps.

The Enchantment of Liquid Spheres

Floating charms in a dance so grand,
Round and plump on ocean's sand.
They bounce and pop with all their might,
Sharing laughter in the moonlight.

A fish with glasses takes a look,
At the merry storybook.
Schools of shrimp giggle in a row,
As bubbles burst with a bubbly glow.

Turtles chuckle, kicking back,
In the silken water, they make a track.
Dolphins leap, making a bet,
Who can pop the fastest yet?

With a splash and a giggle bright,
The sea becomes a stage tonight.
Every dive, a comical play,
As liquid spheres make their way.

Threads of Emotion in Water

Waves weave tales with a splashy thread,
Telling secrets, all joy, no dread.
With a wink and a kick, they entwine,
Painting smiles in the water's shine.

A sea star spins with a dizzy cheer,
Bringing up laughter from those near.
As clams crack jokes in shells so tight,
The ocean echoes with pure delight.

A splash from a shrimp, what a hoot,
Sending ripples in a goofy suit.
With silly dances that make you grin,
Beneath the waves, the fun begins.

As currents flow, emotions rise,
Joy bubbles forth, a sweet surprise.
In the sea's embrace, all feel the same,
Unraveling laughter, a joyful game.

Chasing Shadows Under the Surface

Down where the shadows play and tease,
Wiggly shapes curl in the breeze.
Sneaky fish in a game of chase,
Play tag with a smile, a happy face.

A goby ducked, a flounder peeked,
Under seaweed, they giggled, sneaked.
With every flip and splashy scrap,
The ocean grows a playful map.

A slap of a fin, a giggling tune,
Turns the sea into a silly cartoon.
Shrimps in hats dance a jig,
While whales belly laugh, wiggling big.

Oh what fun beneath the foam,
In the water, they feel at home.
They tumble and grin, oh what a sight,
Chasing giggles in bubbles of light.

The Artistry of Flowing Light

In the depths where giggles dance,
The sunlight plays a twinkling prance.
Fish wear hats, the crabs all cheer,
As jellies float with frothy beer.

Lobsters juggle shells with flair,
Octopus makes a perfect pair.
Giggling waves in a silly spree,
They toast to life beneath the sea.

Seashells giggle, whisper, sigh,
As seahorses twirl in the sky.
With every splash, a laugh is made,
In a world where joy won't fade.

So come and join this wavy ride,
Where laughter flows like the tide.
With quirky friends all around,
In the ocean's heart, joy is found.

Silhouettes Beneath the Waves

Shadows wiggle, shapes collide,
Where the playful creatures hide.
A dolphin dons a pair of shoes,
And seahorses gossip with the blues.

Turtles take a selfie spree,
While starfish pose so quite carefree.
The clownfish crack a joke or two,
Drifting in laughter, all askew.

A treasure chest sings a merry tune,
While crabs dance silly with the moon.
Anemones sway, they're quite the sight,
In this underwater comedic light.

Beneath the waves, the silliness reigns,
As every creature entertains.
With giggles echoing all around,
In ocean depths, pure joy is found.

Ocean-born Reveries of the Mind

In watery dreams where laughter flows,
The otters spin in funny rows.
Starfish jesters laugh and spin,
As bubbles float, and fun begins.

The pufferfish wears a goofy grin,
While hermit crabs play on a whim.
Dancing currents make the scene,
With silly antics, bright and keen.

Coral reefs have jokes to share,
With giggling dolphins everywhere.
In this realm of frolic and play,
Every tide brings a funny day.

So dive into this realm of cheer,
Where every splash brings laughter near.
With whimsical friends in a sea of light,
Life's a joke that feels just right.

Immersed in Daydreams at Sea

In a sea of ideas, bright and wild,
Where sea otters leap like a child.
The fish wear ties and do a dance,
In this quirky, wavy trance.

Seahorses trade silly hats,
While dolphins argue over spats.
Jellyfish float with jolly glee,
In a world where laughter runs free.

Coral castles hold royal jest,
As clownfish put their humor to test.
Merriment blooms like flowers in blue,
In a daydreamed sea, it's all askew.

Let's surf the waves of joyous mirth,
In this funny ocean, spun from birth.
When every ripple tells a joke,
And laughter bubbles like sweet smoke.

Glints of Hope from the Abyss

In the ocean's dark, there's a dance,
Little glimmers twirl with chance.
Fish in tuxedos float with glee,
Waltzing with shrimps, oh what a spree!

An octopus joins with a bow tie,
Twirling 'round as time slips by.
Clams chuckle deep in their shells,
Sharing tales that no one tells.

Starfish gossip on the sea floor,
Planning pranks, oh what a score!
Laughing at the waves that crash,
They throw a party, quite the bash!

Pearls burst out, with jokes to share,
Twinkling charm, beyond compare.
From the depths, a song takes flight,
Echoing laughter into the night.

Ripples of a Hidden Universe

In the quiet tide, secrets play,
Fish tell jokes in a slick ballet.
Octopuses wear hats made of weeds,
While jellyfish float, fulfilling their needs.

A seahorse prances, a sight to behold,
Shaking its tail like it's brave and bold.
Crabs make crustacean puns in the sand,
Comedic chaos, perfectly planned.

Down in the kelp, a party unfolds,
With seaweed snacks that never get cold.
Electric eels bring the dance floor vibes,
Shocking the crowd, oh what fun jibes!

And up in the waves, laughter breaks free,
Dolphins diving, as happy as can be.
In this world, where laughter flows,
Life's an adventure, everybody knows.

The Amplitude of Submerged Thought

Thoughts rise up like bubbles of air,
Twisting and turning without a care.
In a coral maze, the ideas swirl,
Tickling minds like an underwater whirl.

A sand dollar sings with a voice so small,
Echoing dreams that enrapture us all.
With each splash of foam, the laughter ignites,
Surfacing hopes in seawater delights.

Blowfish puff up to share their view,
Filling the room with a humorous hue.
Anemones giggle, swaying with grace,
As sardines form a laughter-filled space.

From this depth, where the silly reigns,
Ideas float freely, like bright champagne.
Inside this abyss, merriment grows,
Hidden treasures, as humor bestows.

Enigmas of Oceanic Light

In the gloom, a flicker, a whimsical sight,
Creatures convene in the soft ocean light.
A whale whispers secrets with a chuckle,
While sea turtles giggle, bursting their bubble.

Anemones play peek-a-boo with the rays,
Tickling the fish in their playful displays.
Clownfish jest, swapping their clothes,
Dressed up for fun, nobody knows!

The krill throw a bash beneath shimmering tide,
And crabbers parade with puffs of pride.
Glimmers of jocularity stretch down below,
While laughter bubbles, like a lively show.

In this ocean, where jests intertwine,
Life is a joke, and the punchline divine.
With mysteries wrapped in comedic flair,
The ocean's enigmas keep us all rare.

Spheres of Laughter Underwater

Under the waves, a giggle floats,
As fish wear hats, like funny coats.
They tumble and spin, in silly dance,
Chasing each other in a bubbly trance.

A crab tells a joke, but it's hard to hear,
With bubbles that pop, and fish guffaw near.
A seaweed wig flies back and forth,
Making a splash, of comedic worth.

Dolphins dive down, their snouts in the air,
Tickling each other without a care.
An octopus juggles, what a sight,
Sea laughter erupts, oh what a delight!

The sea is a stage for laughter and cheer,
In coral costumes, the antics appear.
With funny fish faces, they all engage,
In this underwater wacky, funny page.

The Glistening Layer of Silence

Amidst the quiet, a bubble breaks,
A silent laugh that the ocean makes.
Anemones quiver, they can't help but sway,
Watching the antics, in their own playful way.

A clam tries to sing, but it just clicks,
The starfish all giggle, with their own tricks.
Though the depth is still, there's a joy so clear,
In this layered laughter, we all persevere.

Jellyfish float with a whimsical grace,
While crabs in tuxedos, bask in the space.
The silence is gleaming, yet filled with glee,
In the dance of the deep, there's pure jubilee.

As bubbles rise up, the giggles abound,
In this layer of calm, laughter is found.
Under the surface, where secrets seep,
In the glistening quiet, there's joy to keep.

Echoes from the Ocean Floor

Hear that sound from the depths below?
It's laughter echoing, don't you know?
The fish throw a party, with shrimp as the band,
Dancing on rocks, in a merry land.

A sea turtle winks, sporting a grin,
With dolphins making faces, let the fun begin.
Amongst the seaweed, the humor swells,
As shells share stories, with giggles and yells.

The grouper cracks jokes, just out of sight,
With pufferfish puffing, adding to delight.
Echoing laughter in bubbles of fun,
On the ocean floor, where the jokes have begun.

In this underwater stage, no need for a score,
The laughter keeps rising, hear it roar!
With creatures of whimsy, under the waves,
Echoes of joy, in the beauty it paves.

Gossamer Orbs of Aquatic Wonder

In the blue whispers, orbs gently sway,
Crafting a tale of the underwater play.
With gossamer joy, the fish spin and twirl,
In this magical world, where giggles unfurl.

The seahorses jump, in jubilant leaps,
With laughter so bright, it quite loudly creeps.
An underwater ring, a mysterious sight,
Filling the currents with sheer delight.

An urchin tells tales, its spines a crown,
The starfish applauding, turning upside down.
In this vast expanse, silliness reigns,
With spirits so light, like a dance in the chains.

Gossamer dreams float in this school,
As joyful creatures make laughter the rule.
Under the sea, where wonder is spun,
In orbs of joy, we dance and run.

Celestial Plumes of the Sea

In the ocean's green abyss, fish wear wigs,
Flipping fins in outfits, oh what gigs!
Jellybeans dance, in gowns so bright,
They twirl and they swirl, a comical sight.

A crab with a tie, he's quite the sight,
Telling seashell jokes, all day and night.
Starfish laugh, with arms spread wide,
As the sea cucumbers glide with pride.

Octopi juggling with their many limbs,
Tickle fish laugh, with joy that brims.
The seaweed sways to a merry tune,
As the dolphins groove, beneath the moon.

So take a dip in laughter's embrace,
Where the ocean sings with a lighthearted grace.
With each playful wave and swirling spin,
The joy of the sea, where giggles begin.

Submerged Dreams and Floating Voices

In the twilight depths, the seahorses prance,
Wearing tiny boots, they lead a dance.
With bubbles of laughter, they float on by,
Tickled by currents that giggle and sigh.

Fish in tuxedos play card games galore,
Shuffling through kelp, forever wanting more.
The clams roll their eyes at the silly fish,
While crafting wild tales, they all wish.

A parrotfish sings in a croaky tone,
Making the sandcastles wobble and moan.
While shrimp tell tall tales of giant foes,
In rhymes and in riddles, where nonsense flows.

So dive into dreams, where the oddities gleam,
In currents of laughter, wild and supreme.
With voices of bubbles, the fun never stops,
As the ocean's a stage where the wild whimsy hops.

Enigmatic Ripples

The water ripples with secrets untold,
As sea turtles weave through legends of old.
With googly eyes, they watch and they blink,
While fish sip on tea from a coral sink.

Anemones tickle, while clownfish complain,
As they dodge all the bubbles that swirl like rain.
Starfish wear glasses, pretending to read,
As the sea snails gossip, planting their seed.

The manta ray glides, a graceful ballet,
Chasing jellyfish like they're here to play.
With laughter erupting from creatures below,
The ocean's a circus, with a comical show.

So let the waves carry your frowns far away,
In the kingdom beneath, where the creatures play.
With each splash and giggle, let joy take flight,
In the depths of the sea, where everything's bright.

Glittering Echoes of the Ocean

The waves clink and clatter, like jewels on a string,
As the fish strut their stuff, all ready to bling.
Barnacles gossip, with shells turned in glee,
In the echoing laughter of the deep blue sea.

Crabs on stilts march, with cannonball flair,
While the rays paint their fins with a shimmery dare.
A chorus of bubbles, in symphonic cheer,
Sings songs of a life, adorably queer.

The squids start a band, with tentacles tight,
Playing tunes to the stars that twinkle at night.
With laughter and joy, they sway with a beat,
In the glow of the reef, life feels so sweet.

So dive into mirth, where the echoes resound,
In the whimsical waters where joy can be found.
With shimmering beats and a splash of delight,
The depths of the ocean are vibrant and bright.

Secrets from the Ocean's Veil

In the depths where laughter sways,
Fish wear hats on sunny days.
Octopuses dance with a silly spin,
While crabs play hide-and-seek with a grin.

Turtles zoom in slow-motion grace,
Dolphins giggle with a splashy trace.
Seahorses trot in a wiggly line,
Underwater pranks are simply divine!

Jellyfish float like balloons in flight,
Fancy a waltz in the soft moonlight.
Whales can't help but laugh quite loud,
Their tales a funny underwater crowd.

With coral castles and kelp's cozy nook,
Every nook's a twist in the funny book.
Secrets whisper with a bubbly peak,
Ocean's jests leave us all weak!

Insight from the Submerged

Down below where the silliness shrouds,
Fish wear pajamas and swim with crowds.
Bearded clams hold talent shows at night,
While scallops flash colors—a shimmering sight.

Gullible squids in a game of bluff,
A whirl of ink when the jokes get tough.
Starfish giggle with arms in embrace,
Tickling sea cucumbers in a race.

Lobsters joke about their rather grand meals,
With tales of the sharks that sent them heels.
Even the rocks have stories to share,
Of calamities clad in the ocean's flair.

So dive into laughter's warm current flow,
Where sea creatures gather, and good times grow.
Life when submerged is a quirky delight,
Where jesters of the deep shine ever so bright.

Translucent Portals of Wonder

Through crystal panes where mischief blooms,
Glimpses of laughter from dark ocean rooms.
Sardines wear scarves in a trendy way,
And seagulls play games with the fish every day.

The tangles of seaweed become a grand stage,
While shrimp are the stars of this undersea page.
With boisterous waves and giggles galore,
Every tide brings a new prank to explore.

A clam's grand surprise, a shell on the run,
Slipping and sliding, having too much fun.
Dancing sea sponges with hats made of foam,
In the swirling depths, they find a home.

Join in the frolic, let your worries cease,
In oceans of wonder, where laughter won't freeze.
Through translucent portals, adventure awaits,
In a world full of frolic, and silly plates.

The Mirage Beneath the Waves

A shimmer of laughter beneath frothy sways,
Where fish tell jokes in the sun's warm rays.
A clownfish giggles in a rainbow hue,
While grouper play hide-and-seek, too!

In the sandy nooks, where mermaids reside,
They throw surprise parties with shells as their guide.
They whisper secrets to the turtles so wise,
Who chuckle and roll their trusting eyes.

Barnacles boast of their scruffy old homes,
While anemones bounce to the sound of their gnomes.
The thrill of the catch, the pull of the reel,
Underwater chuckles are far too surreal.

In the mirage beneath, joy's here to stay,
With each swish and giggle, come join the play.
So dive headfirst into this whimsical show,
And float with the laughter that dances below!

Wandering Colors in the Current

A fish in stripes, oh what a sight,
Swirling with giggles, swimming in delight.
A wiggly worm wears a tiny crown,
Chasing bright colors all over town.

With bubbles of laughter, they twist and drift,
Snapping at shadows, it's quite the gift.
The seaweed dances, a silly cheer,
Making everyone burst into sheer gear.

Glimmers of sunlight, a wink from above,
Tickling each scale, like a playful shove.
Squids shoot ink, in a giggling spree,
Creating rain clouds that swim with glee.

A jellyfish juggles with utmost grace,
While crabs do the cha-cha in a funny race.
All of this laughter bubbles through the tide,
Where joy is the catch, and fun is the ride.

Celestial Whispers from Below

In the depths, a party, oh what a scene,
Starfish spin tales, while sea snails glean.
A lobster with glasses gives life advice,
While octopuses wear ties that look quite nice.

Messages from shells send echoes so sweet,
As clams crack jokes, with a rhythmic beat.
Winking sea cucumbers, oh what a sight,
Under the moon's glow, their laughter's light.

A seahorse gallops, with a curious flair,
Telling tall tales of fish in mid-air.
Giggles from dolphins swirl around the bay,
Making waves that dance, in a funny ballet.

With bright twinkling fish floating by,
They share cosmic dreams that never run dry.
Under the ocean, joy takes the lead,
In hearts that are light, and laughter indeed.

Airborne Echoes of the Deep

From the ocean's floor, to skies up high,
Fish throw their hats, each one a sly guy.
A pelican chuckles, a fish in its beak,
Squealing and squirming, it's a funny streak.

Seagulls dive down, for a taste of the tease,
Splashing around like they're dancing with ease.
The tide keeps on whispering jokes in the air,
As crabs crack a grin, with hilarious flair.

Pelicans balance on wobbly mates,
With snacks in their throats that lead to near fates.
Swimmers nearby snort with laughter and glee,
As fishes perform in their sea-faring spree.

The ocean throws parties that last all night,
With splashy surprises and everything light.
Echoes of fun ricochet through the scene,
As everyone's laughing, it's quite the routine.

Haunting Reflections in the Tide

A mirror of mischief, the waves play tricks,
Where goblins of kelp ride on fishy sticks.
The surface is painted with giggles and sighs,
As strange little shadows waltz 'neath the skies.

Grinning at seahorses that dance in a whirl,
While dolphins pirouette, giving a twirl.
A mirage of sillies floats soft on the skin,
Marking the spot where the laughter begins.

Pellets of humor bounce under the foam,
As crabs tell tall tales from the comfort of home.
A riddle from starfish flutters through waves,
Leaving all sea pals in giggles and raves.

Moonbeams curl gently around fish so bright,
As mysteries linger through the magical night.
Reflections of joy shimmer far and wide,
In this quirky kingdom, all silly and tried.

Whispers of the Sunken

In a world where fish can giggle,
And mermaids play hide and seek,
Jellyfish throw a wibbly wiggle,
While seaweed sways, so chic.

Octopuses tell tales of old,
With tentacles all in a twist,
They'll tickle you; it's quite bold,
If you think you can resist!

Crabs dance sideways, full of glee,
Wearing hats made of clams and pearls,
They'll share their secret recipe,
For the best seaweed swirls.

Anemones chuckle with delight,
As they tickle the fish that pass,
In this underwater comic night,
The ocean's all one big laugh!

Effervescence Beneath the Waves

Under waves where laughter flows,
Tiny bubbles bounce around,
Fish wear smiles, striking poses,
As they glide without a sound.

Turtles spin like disco balls,
Waving at the passing squid,
Eels do flips, then take their falls,
While dolphins cheer, all brightly hid.

Starfish count their friends at play,
Chasing plankton in a race,
With every laugh that swims away,
They leave the sea a joyful space.

In this realm of silly scenes,
Where laughter bubbles up with cheer,
The creatures weave a world of dreams,
So come on down, there's fun down here!

Shimmers in the Abyss

Beneath the gloom where light peeks in,
Fishes sport a clownish grin,
With glowing fins that wave and sway,
They turn the dark to bright ballet.

A whale sings silly, off-key tunes,
While crabs compete in silly prunes,
Seahorses ride on bubbles' back,
But watch out for the cephalopac!

The anglerfish boasts of its glow,
While rockfish giggle, putting on a show,
With wriggly dances and knee-slapping moves,
To the rhythm of the ocean grooves.

In depths where sparkles twist and twirl,
The laughter of the sea takes flight,
For under the waves, this hidden world,
Is filled with joy both day and night!

Dancing in the Depths

In waters deep where giggles play,
The fish assemble for a dance,
With flippers flailing all the way,
They prance around in playful trance.

The sea cucumbers sway and glide,
Joining in with joyful grace,
While squids spin and twist with pride,
In this hilarious underwater place.

Pufferfish pop, then laugh out loud,
As the sea horses dive and dive,
They bring their friends, a lively crowd,
Under waves, they feel so alive!

So if you hear the ocean's cheer,
And wonder what's this happy fuss,
Just know that friendship blooms down here,
In depths where laughter rests with us!

Breaths of the Blue Embrace

Down in the ocean, fish do prance,
With giggles and glee, they take a chance.
A tiny crab wears a hat too big,
Dancing around like a silly pig.

A seahorse twirls in a gleaming spin,
While octopuses juggle with a grin.
They tickle the seaweed, start a race,
In a bubble race, they lose with grace.

A dolphin dives in and starts to sing,
Splashing the water, it's a joyous fling.
With tails that flip and roll in delight,
The ocean's a stage, oh, what a sight!

The starfish claps in its own little way,
While turtles play tag, oh, what a day!
In this realm, laughter never ceases,
Under the waves, joy simply increases.

Secrets of the Liquid Realm

Down where the shadows mingle and dance,
A lobster prances in a bright red pants.
With fins that flutter, the mackerels play,
Making the most of a watery day.

A clownfish jests with a wink and a whirl,
While shrimps do the hustle, giving a twirl.
The pufferfish floats with a cheeky puff,
"Is anybody ready for a laugh or a huff?"

The corals blush in the bright ocean light,
As sardines shimmer, all silver and bright.
They giggle in schools, with a splashy cheer,
Tickling the tails of all creatures near.

With tales of treasure and wonders to share,
The lagoon echoes with laughter in air.
In this liquid realm, mischief's a sport,
Diving in joy, like a bubbly report.

Subaquatic Serenades

In the depths where the dolphins take flight,
   Squids start a band, oh, what a sight!
With shells as instruments, tunes fill the sea,
   Each note a splash, with glee and decree.

   A turtle taps softly in funky beat,
     While jellyfish dance, oh-so fleet.
   The anemones sway in a rhythm divine,
     As crabs clap their claws in perfect time.

   A fish in a bowtie does a little jig,
     Spreading his fins, feeling quite big.
   The crowd goes wild, a chorus of cheer,
In this watery concert, laughter draws near.

As bubbles rise high, they join in the fun,
   With laughter echoing till day is done.
Serenades float in the blue's gentle sway,
Beneath the surface, the joys come to play.

Luminescent Fables of the Tide

In the shimmer of dusk, where the fishes' glow,
A pirate octopus puts on a show.
With jokes and jests, he charms all who see,
In the tales spun deep, oh, let it be free!

A sea cucumber shares secrets anew,
While the plankton giggle in their shimmering crew.
The truth is, dear friends, in the ocean's embrace,
Even the whiting can't help but laugh at its face.

With strokes of bright color through kelp they glide,
An eel tells a story — a whimsical ride!
In this watery world, where wonders unfold,
Laughter is currency, more precious than gold.

With waves that chuckle and tides that tease,
Under the moonlight, the ocean's at ease.
Every ripple whispers of joy and delight,
In luminescent fables, all creatures unite.

The Lullaby of Watery Dreams

In the pond where fish do stare,
Float a chorus without a care.
Jellybeans on wobbly waves,
Giggling fins and flippered knaves.

Whimsical ripples, a splashy song,
Dancing bubbles that bounce along.
Turtles chuckle, seals take a dive,
Underwater jesters, oh what a hive!

Amidst the seaweed's leafy sways,
Charming pranks in watery bays.
A clam that claps, a crab that croons,
Silly shanties sung to the moons.

Where laughter lurks in every crest,
Even the octopus takes a rest.
Mariners tickled by zephyr's tease,
Chuckling through the gentle breeze.

Delight in the Liquid Embrace

Wobbling ships on a sea of glee,
Bubblegum waves that dance with me.
Fish in bow ties, all dressed to play,
Swaying sea stars on bright display.

Lobsters laugh in their crustacean suits,
Crabs doing jiggles in tiny boots.
A dolphin dives with a whoop and a gig,
While otters play catch with a squishy twig.

Sea cucumbers sing silly songs,
In this world where laughter belongs.
Eels that wiggle and socks that swim,
Chasing the tide on a whimsy whim.

With every splash, there's joy to find,
The ocean's heart, so sweet and kind.
In this dance beneath a sunny sky,
Even the seaweed starts to fly.

Fathoms of Floating Fantasies

In the depths where the seafoam plays,
Giggling fish in a bubble ballet.
A shark with a smile and a wink so sly,
Wearing a bowler that makes fish fly.

Clams are gossiping, full of pride,
While seahorses shuffle side to side.
Octopus painting with colors so bright,
Chasing his dreams through the inky night.

A whale's rumble is a ticklish tune,
As mermaids dance 'neath the silvery moon.
With every splash, a new joke's spun,
Fathoms of fun, oh what a run!

Turtles glide like they're on a slide,
Eels doing tricks with a twist of pride.
In this watery world, where laughter's the key,
Even the sea anemones giggle with glee.

The Pulse of the Dark Sea

In shadows where the lanterns glow,
Giggles echo, a soft undertow.
Anglerfish grin with illuminating charm,
While starfish are balmy, a waving arm.

The jellyfish float in a jelly parade,
Dancing like dreams that won't ever fade.
Grouchy old lobsters with crabby grins,
Grumble and gossip about their fins.

In this murky realm, a cheeky jest,
A sponge wearing glasses, oh what a fest!
With whispers of tickles from currents that sway,
The ocean's alive with a laugh every day.

So dive in deep for a playful treat,
Humorous secrets in every heartbeat.
In the pulse of the dark, bright wit will sprout,
Where every splash invites joyous about.

Underwater Reveries of the Mind

A fish with a hat swims by with glee,
Chasing a crab who shimmies free.
A turtle plays poker, a whale's his dealer,
As jellyfish dance, it's quite the meal-er!

An octopus juggles a handful of seashells,
While seahorses play out their own funny tales.
The starfish cheers, waving its arms,
"Come join our party; it's filled with charms!"

The coral hums songs of laughter and cheer,
As snails in monocles sip on some beer.
A dolphin does backflips, a sight to behold,
In this underwater realm, let the stories unfold!

So dive in with joy, give a splash and a shout,
In this world of wonders, there's never a doubt.
With whimsy and giggles, let's frolic and play,
In this magical ocean, we'll dance all day!

Shattered Thoughts in the Surf

A clam opens wide, and swallows its grin,
While crabby old codgers to gossip begin.
The seaweed sways with a life of its own,
While minnows all giggle at shells they have blown.

A shark with a smile just wants to befriend,
While jellybeans bob in the waves without end.
The barnacles clank like a band gone awry,
As puffers puff up and float on by.

A narwhal with glasses recites all the quips,
And otters perform their synchronized flips.
A whale hums a tune, well, sort of off-key,
Yet everyone dances, so wild and so free!

So let's ride the swells, with laughter and cheer,
In this splashy circus, there's nothing to fear.
With each wave we float, may our spirits unite,
In this frothy adventure, oh what a delight!

The Symmetry of Swirling Dreams

A squid with a monocle draws on the sand,
While fishies in bow ties do form a cool band.
Clownfish crack jokes that would make you beam,
In this swirl of colors, it's quite the scene.

Anemones giggle as bubbles they blow,
While crabs play charades, putting on quite a show.
With each wave that rolls, the laughter will swell,
In this dance of the depths, all's well that ends well!

A starfish taps toes to the rhythm of light,
While turtles in tuxedos conduct the night.
The anglerfish flashes its glamorous grin,
As sea creatures waltz, let the fun now begin!

So join in the chaos, embrace the surprise,
In this ocean of dreams, where the silly flies.
With whimsy and wonder, we'll make our own theme,
In this underwater ballet, we'll twirl and we'll gleam!

Rhythm of the Deep Blue

A dolphin with dreams of becoming a star,
Sings tunes while performing in front of the car.
Octopus maracas shake with such flair,
As squids coordinate a colorful fair.

Seahorses trot in with a glittery glide,
They twirl and they spin, oh, what joy they provide!
With every bright splash, a new jest appears,
In this festive frenzy, let's banish our fears.

A crab in a bowler disputes with a fish,
Who claims that his lunch is a rather big dish.
While seafans swish softly, taking it slow,
The reef is alive with such chatter and glow!

So join the parade in this watery spree,
Let laughter resound from each creature so free.
For in these blue depths, with whimsical style,
We'll dance through the currents, and laugh all the while!

Hidden Laughter in Dark Waters

In the quiet depths, a giggle plops,
A fish with a bowtie does somersault hops.
Octopus clowns juggle shiny seaweed,
While jellyfish dance, oh what a deed!

Gurgling sounds echo, a playful tease,
Crabs in a conga with crusty old knees.
Sea turtles chuckle with shells all a-glow,
While lobsters tell tales of a ticklish toe!

Coral reefs chortle, in colors so bright,
A chorus of chuckles entertains the night.
The playful parade of the ocean's delight,
Where laughter swims by with a twinkling light!

And with every splash, joy's rhythm is spun,
In the depths where the ticklish waters run.
Each wave that passes, a joke that you'll keep,
Within swirling tides, lies laughter so deep!

Reflections of Forgotten Tales

In murky corners where shadows yawn,
Old tales unfold with a glimmering dawn.
A dolphin whispers secrets with flair,
While pirate fish giggle at what they wear.

Merfolk weave stories with musical fins,
Laughing at sailors' old, silly sins.
Starfish hold court with a wink and a nod,
As seahorses prance, quite frankly, they're odd!

Anemones pulse, in a bubbly sway,
Echoing laughter from long gone days.
With every reflection that shimmers and glints,
A reminder that joy often lies in the prints.

So here in the depths, where the silly reside,
Memories tickle like a whimsical tide.
Each flicker of light, every tale gives a peep,
Of laughter that lingers, and dreams that won't sleep!

The Soft Song of Submarine Bliss

Under the waves, where the soft currents flow,
A calypso of giggles begins to bestow.
With clams playing harp, and fish keeping time,
A rhythm emerges, a joyous mime.

Goblins of seaweed sway to the beat,
While stingrays float by with a tap of their feet.
A conch shell's whisper, a melody sweet,
Underwater parties, a bubbly retreat!

Seashells are shakers, making sounds oh-so clear,
A dance of delight, as laughter draws near.
With whirlpools spinning in a whimsical twist,
Every splash adds to the sweet, silly list.

So dive into joy, let the waves take you high,
In this wet, merry land, where no one says bye.
As bubbles burst softly, and giggles persist,
With each tune that rises, a snicker exists!

Liquid Light and Whispering Currents

When sunlight pours down through the rippling tides,
The sea sprays a canvas where mischief resides.
With dolphins on skateboards and turtles on swings,
The ocean's a circus of splendid odd things!

Little fish giggle at a whale's silly dance,
And sea cucumbers dance in a slow, clumsy prance.
With bubbles like giggles that tickle the air,
The joyous commotion, a party to share!

Coral reefs chuckle, as currents purr soft,
The rhythm of laughter, where all spirits loft.
Nautical naughtiness, in splashes and swirls,
Every twinkling wave holds bright, funny whirls.

So join in the fun in this underwater spree,
Where laughter and light create whimsical glee.
Just slip on your flippers, you'll float without care,
In a world of delight, where happiness is rare!

www.ingramcontent.com/pod-product-compliance
Lightning Source LLC
Chambersburg PA
CBHW060144230426
43661CB00003B/563